HARD-WON VICTORY

The Canadians at Ortona, 1943

by
N. M. Christie

Access to History No. 7

CEF BOOKS
2001

National Library of Canada Cataloguing in Publication Data
Christie, N.M.
  Hard-won victory: the Canadians at Ortona, 1943
(Access to history series; no.7)
Includes bibliographical references.
ISBN 1-896979-40-8
  1. Ortona (Italy), Battle of, 1943. 2. World War, 1939-1945 — Campaigns — Italy. 3. Canada, Canadian Army, Canadian Infantry Division, 1ST — History. 4. World War, 1939-1945 — Regimental histories — Canada. I. Title. II. Series: Access to History series (Ottawa, Ont.); no. 7.

D763. I82O77 2001   940.54'215713   C2001-901946-7

Published by:
  CEF BOOKS
  PO BOX 40083,
  OTTAWA, ONTARIO K1V 0W8
  613-823-7000

This book is dedicated to the memory of the 110,000 Canadians who willingly gave their lives in the defence of freedom in the Twentieth Century.
Lest We Forget

Acknowledgements:
  We would like to thank Ontario Command of The Royal Canadian Legion and the Department of Canadian Heritage for the support which made this series possible. Additional thanks to Mr. Earl Kish, Dr. Reg Roy, and Mr. Brian McClean for their valuable contributions to this book.

**Publication of this book
has been supported by
the Canadian War Museum.**

Front cover: Sniper Jack Bailey of Stratford, Ontario, aims towards the town of Orsogna, Italy, January 1944.
(PAC PA130609)
Back cover: Harry Mayerovitch, 1943.

"The very smell of death and destruction reached us in the orange grove, communicating its sanguinary message. A holocaust of red glowed in the sky, revealing a ragged skyline as tongues of flame leapt into the night. We peered through the trembling darkness from a ring contour overlooking the awesome sight. Down-wind from the action the frightful intimate sounds of battle were all too clear, bursts of automatic fire, the Bren and the Schmeisser answering one another, each with its own distinguishing accent. A dozen concurrent dialogues penetrated the blunter, duller, but more profound thunder of the gunning. From the intervening vineyards rose a ghostly vapour, like a shroud winding itself about the town. The most boisterous and profane among us became silent in face of what we witnessed. The morbid fascination of destruction held us in its grip as life and its moments dissolved before our eyes. Over all, the deafening voice of guns beat a massive dirge like the unmuffled drums of hell."

Charles Comfort, Canadian War Artist,
Written overlooking Ortona, December 1943.

The Make-up of an Army

The Army - An Army was made-up of a number of Army Corps, usually between three and five, and could number up to 300,000 men. During 1943 the Canadians were part of the Eighth Army. The Eighth Army consisted of fighting units from Britain, India, New Zealand and in 1944, from Greece, Poland and Italy. In 1943 it was commanded by the British General, Bernard Montgomery. An Army Group was one or more Armies under one command, under the control of a Field-Marshal.

The Army Corps - An Army Corps consisted of a number of Infantry and Armoured Divisions, depending on its needs. Consequently its numeric strength varied, but it could put as many as 125,000 men in the field. Primarily an administrative unit, the Army Corps wasresponsible for a specific operation. It was commanded by a Lieutenant-General. The Canadians belonged to a couple of Corps in 1943, the 13th British and later the 5th Corps.

The Division - There were two types of Divisions; Armoured and Infantry. An Infantry Division consisted of three Infantry Brigades, each contained three Infantry Regiments (or Battalions), machine-gun units, field ambulances, engineers, signals and a variety of artillery. It was a self-contained unit, and was composed of 18,500 men. An Armoured Division was smaller at 15,000 men. It had one armoured brigade of three Armoured Regiments, a Brigade of three infantry regiments and a variety of support troops, including motorized transport, repair, artillery, medical, signals, etc. Both units were commanded by a Major-General.

The Brigade - The Infantry Brigade consisted of three infantry regiments, and supporting troops, medics, signallers, etc., and totalled about 3,500 men. An Armoured Brigade was made-up of three armoured regiments of 60 tanks each, as well as its support units. A Brigade was commanded by a Brigadier-General.

The Battalion - An Infantry Battalion or Regiment consisted of 850 men. It is commanded by a Lieutenant-Colonel. It was broken into four rifle Companies, a Support company and a Headquarters Company. A rifle Company was commanded by a Major or Captain. Each Company was broken down into three Platoons, commanded by a Lieutenant, and each Platoon was broken down into three sections, commanded by a Sergeant.

Table of Contents

Order of Battle - The Canadian Army - Italy, 1943

1st Canadian Infantry Division
4th Reconnaissance (Princess Louise Dragoon Guards) Regiment
Machine-Guns - The Saskatoon Light Infantry

1st Infantry Brigade	**2nd Infantry Brigade**	**3rd Infantry Brigade**
The Royal Canadian Regiment	Princess Patricia's Canadian Light Infantry	Royal 22e Regiment
The Hastings and Prince Edward Regiment	The Seaforth Highlanders of Canada	The Carleton and York Regiment
48th Highlanders of Canada	The Loyal Edmonton Regiment	The West Nova Scotia Regiment

An Infantry Division also included five Regiments of Artillery, four companies of Engineers, and three Field Ambulances.

It consisted at full strength, which was rarely the case, of 18,347 men. The Division was equipped with 12,265 pistols and rifles, 1,302 machine guns, 359 mortars, 436 Anti-tank projectors (PIATs), 307 artillery guns, and 3,347 vehicles of a variety of sizes and types. The Reconnaissance Regiment was equipped with Armoured cars.

1st Canadian Armoured Brigade

11th Armoured (Ontario) Regiment
12th Armoured (Three Rivers) Regiment
14th Armoured (The Calgary) Regiment

The Armoured Brigade had roughly 5,000 men. Each Armoured Regiment had 60 tanks. The principal tank used by the Canadians in Italy was the Sherman.

Introduction

The first years of the war had been quiet ones for Canada's soldiers. Since 1939 Canadians had been arriving by the thousands in England, in fact 176,000 Canadian soldiers were there by the end of 1942. Yet they had seen little action. They had spent a quiet war and while others fought in North Africa and in the Far East, they sat in their camps, trained and waited. In July 1943 their long wait ended. They would be part of a major enterprise, the first attack on Adolf Hitler's Fortress Europe.

Until that eventful day in 1943 the war had not been a good one for the Canadian Army. They had been involved in only two battles. A small Canadian force had been sent to Hong Kong in 1941. In December a large Japanese force captured the old British Colony and all of Canada's 2,000 troops were killed or captured. They had lasted a mere month. At Dieppe in 1942 a force of 5,000 Canadians attacked the French seaport of Dieppe. Dieppe was a fiasco for the attackers and only 2,000 men returned. The others were killed or taken prisoner. These failures, which were not the fault of the Canadians themselves, none-the-less had planted seeds of doubt.

In Canada the public was disturbed by Dieppe and Hong Kong, and they were disturbed even more by the inactivity of the Canadian Army. The newspapers would arrive daily, and the headlines would reveal the great Allied battles in North Africa, in Russia, the daring exploits of the Royal Canadian Air Force and Royal Canadian Navy, but never a word on the Army. It was time for action and all Canadians knew it.

On July 1st, 1943, under a veil of secrecy, a force of 26,000 Canadian troops boarded their transport ships in England and embarked on a precarious journey through submarine-infested waters for the Mediterranean. It was only then they were informed they were to be part of an Allied invasion force. Their objective was to capture Sicily, and knock Hitler's Axis ally, Italy, out of the war.

Over the next few months the Allies would fight a brutal and difficult campaign against a determined and experienced enemy. They would capture Sicily, and weeks later invade the boot of Italy. In their first real fighting Canada would be there, fighting alongside American, British, Indian, New Zealander, Polish, and French soldiers. Together they would turn the tide of the war.

Through the early days of the fighting, first in Sicily and then in Italy, Canada's soldiers would be toughened by the battles they fought. But it was not until December 1943 that they would be given the task that would prove to themselves and their Allies that the Canadians could fight with the best of them. It was in the fields and gullies near a picturesque fishing town on the Adriatic coast, called Ortona, that their hardest test would come. In a month of heavy combat, with small groups of soldiers pitted against one another, they would meet and defeat some of Nazi Germany's toughest troops. Canada's men would face a battle where success could only come from courage and tenacity and it was here that Canada gained its first hard-won victory.

Recruiting Poster, 1941.
(E. Aldwinkle and E. Cloutier)

The World at War, 1939-1943

The outbreak of the Second World War in September 1939 pitted the old European enemies against each other. Once again, as in 1914, it was the Allies, France and the British Empire (including Canada, India, South Africa, New Zealand and Australia) against Germany, in a war considered as "Round Two" of the First World War. There were strategic differences from 1914. Italy sided with Nazi Germany and formed an alliance known as the Axis Powers. The World's largest countries, the United States and Soviet Russia, were neutral.

The two sides were stalemated through the winter of 1939 into the spring of 1940, until Germany suddenly attacked and defeated France and drove the British off the continent. By the end of 1940 Germany dominated Europe, and Britain and her Empire was all that stood between Hitler and domination of most of the World.

In the summer of 1941 Hitler attacked Soviet Russia. In North Africa British troops were fighting the Italians. In December 1941 the Japanese, who had secretly joined the Axis, attacked British, Dutch and American bases in the Far East. In six months the face of the war had changed completely. Britain now had two important new Allies, Soviet Russia and the United States. However the war was going badly. At the end of 1941 and well into 1942 the Axis Powers crushed the Allies on every front. In North Africa Italian-German forces pushed the British into Egypt. In Russia the Nazis drove 1,600 km to the gates of Moscow, destroying Soviet armies in their path and capturing millions. In the Far East the Japanese defeated British, Australian and American forces in Burma, Singapore and the Philippines and were threatening Australia with invasion. By the end of 1942 it appeared the Soviets were beaten. Josef Stalin, the leader of the Soviets, demanded the British and Americans act.

Mounting a Second Front was a major undertaking whose planning and preparation would take years. Huge quantities of equipment would have to be manufactured and millions of soldiers, sailors and airmen trained and outfitted. The earliest date for the assault was 1944. In the meantime Stalin would have to be satisfied with smaller ventures. In November 1942 a U.S. force landed in North Africa, and in conjunction with the more experienced British troops already fighting there, defeated the Germans and Italians and drove them back across the deserts into Tunisia. The U.S.

troops and their armoured units gained valuable battle experience. In May 1943 the Allies forced the Axis army to surrender in North Africa and took 248,000 German prisoners.

Things were also going better in Russia. In January 1943 the Soviets had inflicted the first major defeat of the war on the Germans. At Stalingrad they had destroyed more than 300,000 Nazi soldiers. In less than six months the tide of war had changed again.

After the victory in North Africa the Allies decided that the next step would be the invasion of Sicily. There were several reasons for choosing Sicily as the next target. The conquest of Sicily would give the Allies complete control of the Mediterranean Sea. It could also deliver the knock-out blow to the struggling Italians, who had long ago lost their stomach for war and were dissatisfied with their fascist leader, Hitler's friend, Benito Mussolini.

The plan called for an amphibious assault along the southern Sicilian coast. The attack would be made with the troops made available by the defeat of the Axis in Africa. There would be one change to the forthcoming offensive: the attacking armies would include 26,000 Canadians.

Canada at War, 1939-1943

Canada had declared war on September 9th, 1939 in aid of Britain. By the end of the year the 1st Canadian Infantry Division, 15,000 strong, was sent to Britain. After the defeat of France in May 1940 the Canadians became the main defence in Britain against a German invasion. By the end of 1940 it became clear the Germans were not going to invade the British Isles and the role of the Canadians became less important. But thousands of Canadian soldiers continued to arrive in the United Kingdom and by December, 1941 125,000 men were stationed there. They trained continually but the inactivity did not help Canadian morale or battle efficiency. While other soldiers of the British Empire (Britain, South Africa, India, Australia, New Zealand) fought valiantly in North Africa, Greece and in the Far East Canada's Army stagnated.

At Hong Kong in December 1941 the Japanese had killed or captured an entire Canadian force of 1,973 men. It was the Canadian Army's first foray in the war and they had suffered 100% casualties.

FORTRESS EUROPE - JUNE 1943

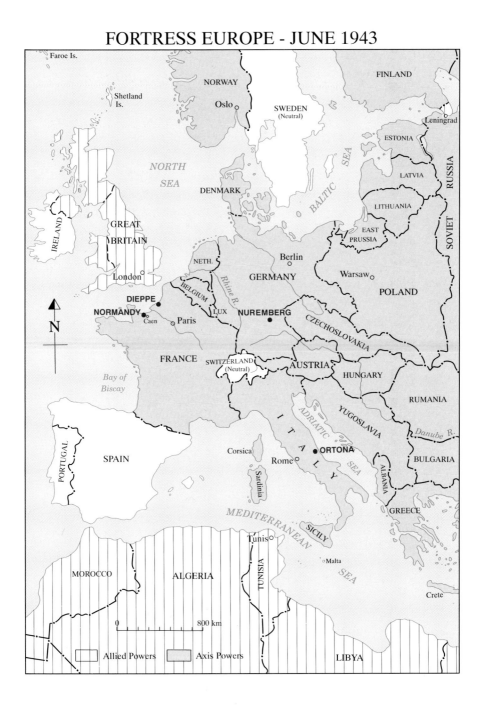

The same was not true of thousands of other Canadians who had enlisted in the Royal Canadian Air Force and the Royal Canadian Navy. The RCAF had been in action since the Battle of Britain in 1940, and Canadian pilots and air crews were in action in every theatre of war. More than 95,000 Canadians were on strength of the RCAF by the end of 1941. The same was true of the RCN. The ships of Canada's navy were constantly in action in the Atlantic Ocean, escorting convoys and hunting German submarines. Both Services had contributed much to the War effort.

The first actions of the Canadian Army were not successful. In 1941 a force of 1,975 inexperienced Canadian soldiers were sent to defend the old British Colony of Hong Kong in case of a Japanese attack. Three weeks after the men arrived the Japanese mounted a massive assault on Hong Kong. After a week's heavy fighting Hong Kong fell, and the entire Canadian force was captured or killed. The next Army operation was August 1942 at Dieppe. Dieppe was a disaster for the force of 5,000 Canadian troops that took part in the Raid. It was a military failure that cost Canada 907 dead and 1,946 captured.

By June 1943, 200,000 Canadian troops were in Britain. Some had been there for four years. They had arrived as teenagers in 1939 and had grown up; many were married and now had families. Canada had always wanted its men to fight as one unit, as they had in the First World War, but the opportunity had never arisen. Finally the Canadian Army was allowed to be broken-up to gain battle experience.

They did not have to wait long for their first assignment. In April 1943 the 1st Canadian Infantry Division and the 1st Canadian Armoured Brigade, a force 26,000 strong, received orders to prepare to move. On July 1st, 1943 they embarked from Scotland for the Mediterranean. Once aboard ship the men were advised that they were to take part in the invasion of Sicily.

"... this will be the Canadians first real operation apart from the Dieppe raid... it is terribly important that it should go well for many reasons - the reputation of Canadian soldiers which stood so high in the last war... and above all the great importance to the future of the war that we should do our share in this particular operation..."
Major-General Guy Simmonds, Commander of the 1st Canadian Division

Operation "Husky"; The Invasion of Sicily, July 1943

The invasion of Sicily was code-named "Husky", and it would involve an American-Anglo-Indian-New Zealander-Canadian Force being landed along the southern coast and an airborne assault against Axis positions just behind the coastal defences. The plan called for the U.S. force to capture the western part of the island and the British Empire forces, the famous Eighth Army, to land on the south-eastern corner of Sicily. The Eighth Army would then push north and capture the ports of Syracuse and Messina.

On July 9th, 1943 the 2,600 ships of the invasion force collected at their rendezvous points and turned for Sicily. Allied aircraft had bombed the major defences in advance of the landings, and as the ships approached they once again attacked the Axis positions. The huge guns of the Navy also added to the pounding. At 2:45 am on July 10th the assault vessels hit the beaches.

As the Allied troops landed they met little opposition. The coast was manned by Italians and the High Command had been right, the Italians had little interest in fighting. The men were often treated as liberators by the Sicilian civilians. All the landings were successful and the invasion of Sicily had started out on a great note.

The Canadians had succeeded in capturing their objectives the first day and had only suffered 75 killed and wounded. Throughout July the Canadians continued to put pressure on the enemy. The troops advanced slowly, fighting all the way, bypassing pockets of resistance if possible. By August 9th the pressure put on the Germans was finally taking its toll. Although the Allied gains were not great they had managed to push the enemy back to an extent that even Adolf Hitler conceded defeat and the evacuation of the Axis forces started. Even with the enemy evacuating, small rear guards still held up the advance. Finally on August 17th, 38 days after the landings, the Americans finally entered Messina. The Sicilian Campaign was over.

The campaign had been a success for the Allies. They had captured the first piece of Hitler's Europe and inflicted 15,000 casualties on the Germans and 139,000 on the Italians of which 137,000 were prisoners. The cost to the Allies was 19,000 killed and wounded. The campaign was not an entire victory however, as 35,000 Germans and 62,000 Italians and much war material had been successfully evacuated. The Allies would have to fight these troops again.

"The Canadians were magnificent in the Sicilian campaign. They had done no fighting before, but they were very well trained and they soon learnt the tricks of the battlefield which count for so much and save so many lives. When I drew them into reserve to prepare for the invasion of the Italian mainland, they had become one of the Eighth Army's veteran divisions."
General Bernard Montgomery, Commanding the Eighth Army, 1943.

For the Canadians Sicily had been an important campaign. Canada's soldiers had gained battle experience and had acquitted themselves well in fighting under such trying conditions. The cost to Canada was comparatively light. They had suffered 2,310 casualties, including 562 dead.

The Political Situation

The invasion of Sicily had gone a long way in knocking Italy out of the war. On July 25th, 1943 the Italians deposed their fascist dictator, Benito Mussolini, and placed him under arrest. A new government was formed that was considered more inclined to surrender, although initially it stated it would continue the war as an ally of Nazi Germany. The Allies felt that one more good knock would finish off the Italians. It would come 17 days after the fall of Sicily, and it would be the invasion of Italy.

There were also political problems in the Allied camp. Many felt the invasion of Italy was not important. They felt all resources and manpower available should be used to prepare for the invasion of France, the real Second Front. To invade Italy would just be wasting resources. To placate them a commitment was made to the invasion of France in 1944 as the top priority, but the attack on Italy was still to go ahead. The main proponent of the Italian Invasion was Winston Churchill, the Prime Minister of Britain. Churchill wanted to finish off the Italians so the Germans would have to move men from Russia to replace them in Yugoslavia, Greece and in Italy itself. It would also provide prime airfields for Allied bombers so they could attack Germany and other strategic targets. In the end, as he usually did, Churchill got his way.

A lesser political problem was also evident between the Allied armies. There was a competition brewing between the U.S. and British. It had been brought to a boil in Sicily, and it continued through the remainder of the war. Canada was caught in the middle. For the rest of the war Canadians were given few of the more prestigious objectives. They were reserved for the Americans or the British in their pursuit of glory.

The Invasion of Italy, September 1943

Italy is 75% mountains and hills. It is a beautiful country. The boot of Italy is roughly 160 km wide, from the Tyrrhenian Sea to the Adriatic Sea. The Apennine mountain range runs the length of the peninsula and gives Italy a rocky spine. The mountains are cut with river valleys and narrow roads meander through them. Small villages nestle high up on the hillsides and in the valleys. In many ways the centre of Italy is much like Sicily, offering the defenders great natural obstacles to blunt any attack. Any movement is limited to the roads and railways which are overseen by the heights that surround them. On each side of the Apennines are rich coastal plains that are cut with ravines and gullies, and dotted with groves of olives and grape vines. Even these pretty coastal plains are unfriendly. The many rivers and canals can slow the best armoured movement and in addition they are closely bounded by the foothills of the mountains. They provide excellent coverage for defenders and allow them to hide and wait for the attackers to move forward. These defences would force any attacker to take the greatest precautions at every bend in the road.

The weather in this region is hot and humid in the summer and rainy, overcast and cold in the fall-winter period. These conditions result in extremes in temperatures, from sweltering heat to frost. The damp from continuous rain makes the colder temperatures bone-chilling, colder than a Prairie winter. The rain brings the mud and floods. Mud can be as great an opponent to armies as their enemy.

In the Italian Campaign all of nature's own would be used against the Allies. In addition the Germans would be adding their own twists to make Italy an even more formidable place.

The Plan

The decision to invade Italy was made in May 1943, before the attack on Sicily had taken place. The final details of the plan would depend on how well the Sicilian campaign went. As the Sicilian Campaign approached its final stages the Allied Generals put in place the details that would bring them back to Europe. The invasion would take place shortly after the fall of Sicily, before the Germans could bring reinforcements to the south and prepare strong defences. The location of any Italian landings would have to be within fighter range or 300 km of the airfields that would be established on Sicily. By mid-July the details of the invasion were decided. It would be a

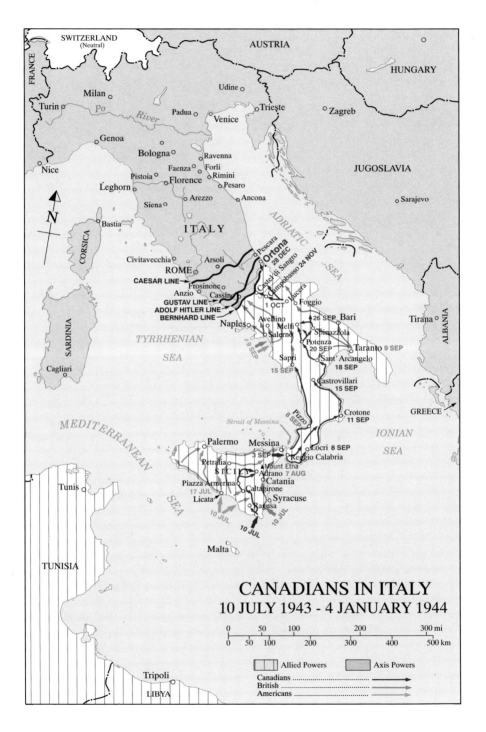

CANADIANS IN ITALY
10 JULY 1943 - 4 JANUARY 1944

0	50	100		200		300 mi
0	50	100	200	300	400	500 km

Allied Powers   Axis Powers

Canadians ....
British ....
Americans ....

two-phase attack. In the initial phase a Canadian-British force would cross the 8 km distance across the Straits of Messina, landing on the beaches on the toe of the Italian Boot. Six days later the Fifth Army, a U.S.-British force would make an amphibious landing near the strategic port of Salerno on the Tyrrhenian Sea, 300 km north of Sicily and 240 km south of the Capital City of Italy, Rome.

The Canadians would land near the small town of Reggio Calabria. They would have the honour of being amongst the first to re-enter Fascist Europe. The problem facing the Generals and their troops landing on the beaches was that they had no idea what sort of reception they would get. Would they be unopposed? Was this the "soft underbelly of the Axis," or would the enemy be waiting for them? They could not count on surprise in this venture. The Germans and Italians knew they were coming.

"I'll never forget Mr. Churchill... standing up at a map of the Mediterranean and pointing to the 'soft underbelly of Europe'... It later became my job to split that soft underbelly and I assure you that I found it a tough old gut."
General Mark Clark, Commanding the Fifth Army.

The Invasion of Italy, September 3rd, 1943

Since the middle of August Allied bombers had continuously bombarded the enemy's railways, transport and communication centres, gun positions and any other defensive works they could find in southern Italy. They had destroyed the Axis air forces and had total dominance of the air. In advance of the sea assaults bombers flew 3,000 missions (sorties) over Italy. The great ships of the Allied navies patrolled up and down the coast blasting targets of opportunity.

In Italy on the night of September 1st/2nd, 1943, the troops allocated for the first wave of the assault boarded the Landing Craft. For Canada the first men to hit the beaches would be from the West Nova Scotia and the Carleton and York Regiments. Just after midnight on September 3rd, 1943, in faint moonlight, the ships headed out. Italy was only a few km away across the calm sea.

At 3:30 am a huge barrage opened up. Artillery fired from positions along the Sicilian coast and the huge guns of the Naval ships added to the inferno, lighting up the coast. At 4:50 am the Landing Craft began the final run.

The Canadians hitting the beach found no opposition. The soldiers ran from the ships and advanced inland. By 8:10 am they had entered and secured the village of Reggio. They found it in a state of total destruction. The artillery had done its job well. Canadian reinforcements were filing from the beaches and moving inland. Men of the Royal 22e Regiment and machine-gunners from the Saskatoon Light Infantry were already pushing on, anxious for some action. Back on the beach more Canadians came ashore. The 48th Highlanders were accompanied in by the sound of bagpipes.

The landing was a complete success. Three thousand prisoners had been captured. The cost to the Canadians was a mere 9 wounded. The opening chapter to the liberation of Europe was a good one.

The British landing a few km away was also a great success. They too had met little opposition and had secured their beachhead. Now for all Allied soldiers the next step was to push on and keep the pressure on the retreating enemy. The only concern to the Allies was where were the Germans?

Italy Surrenders

The British and Canadians continued their pursuit of the Germans and Italians but on September 8th, 1943 the world took a turn for the better. Italy surrendered. Now as the men moved through the Italian villages they were treated as liberators. One of the most important objectives of the invasion of Italy had now been achieved. The only question remained was what would the Nazis do; would they leave Italy and set up a defensive line in the north or would they fight it out metre by metre with an unsurpassed tenacity? The U.S. -British Army landing at Salerno would occur the next morning, September 9th, 1943. The German reaction to the landing would indicate the way they were going to fight.

The Fifth Army Lands at Salerno, September 9th, 1943

The surrender of the Italians had not really surprised the Germans. They had moved thousands of men into Italy in the event of such a situation and although the surrender had caused some anxiety the German Army had quickly moved in to disarm the Italian soldiers and replace them with far better trained and more determined Nazi troops.

In fact the German generals had roughly 100,000 men deployed in southern Italy. Many were held near Naples, only 50 km from where the Fifth Army was going to land.

In the early morning of September 9th the massive armada carrying 100,000 men, tanks, guns and supplies landed on the beaches near Salerno. Allied aircraft covered the skies and huge ships shelled the area. The men thought their task would be an easy one, as had been the British-Canadian landings near Reggio. But they could not have been more mistaken. Their opponents were German and it was clear the Germans would yield no ground. Fierce fighting broke out all around the port.

After two days the Allies had moved only 16 km inland against a ferocious German defence. For several days the Germans held until finally they withdrew to prepared defensive positions south of Rome. The Allied generals now knew what the enemy's plans were going to be. The Nazis would fight for every metre, and do everything in their power to block the road to Rome.

On September 9th, 1943 the British and Canadians were still 300 km away from Salerno. In 12 days they had covered the distance and on the 21st the Fifth and Eighth Armies linked. Now the Allies had firm control of the Italian peninsula from Salerno on the Tyrrhenian Sea to Bari on the Adriatic.

The Canadians resumed their movement by sending mobile patrols towards Foggia, 30 km away. By September 27th the strategic airfields at Foggia fell, and another major objective of the Italian Campaign was now in the bag.

In October the Allies continued to push back the enemy. Naples was taken. The Canadians were in the mountains once again, pushing forward against an unseen opponent. There would be a brief clash then the enemy would withdraw behind another bend in the road or over the next hill. Each encounter succeeded in slowing the Canadian movements, and adding more names to the casualty lists. The advance was continuing but it was getting harder and harder, and the price for every km was being paid in blood. On October 14th, 1943 the First Division captured Compobasso, a town of 17,000 inhabitants, but as the month ground on, the fatigue of constant fighting and marching took its toll, and there was no breakthrough to be seen. There was only more rain and mud and hills and valleys. The month of October, 1943 cost Canada 179 killed and 504 wounded.

"They were bringing in all the dead and laying them out in front of the orderly tent. The smell was bloody awful... They must have been dead for several days as the smell was out of this world... They placed the bodies in a cart and sewed each man up in an army blanket... The Chaplain showed as much respect that he could under the circumstances."
Jack Duggan, Royal Canadian Army Medical Corps.

The Decision to go for Rome

At this point the Italian Campaign, or "the Spaghetti League" as it became known, had achieved most of its objectives at little cost. Italy had been knocked out of the war, and the Allies controlled the Mediterranean, German troops had to be recalled from other fronts to replace the Italians and the Foggia airfields had been captured. Consequently many Allied generals, particularly the Americans, felt there was no need to continue the fighting. To them it was a waste of manpower and war material that could be better employed in the upcoming invasion of France. To Winston Churchill, the British Prime Minister, Rome was an important symbol. Rome was only 100 km away, and he felt, as did others, that the Nazis would give up on Rome and withdraw to defensive positions in the north of Italy. The decision was made. For political reasons the Allies would take the ancient city as soon as possible. Rome became a prestige target.

What they did not know was that to Adolf Hitler, the erratic dictator of Nazi Germany, Rome was also a symbol, and one that would be held. Denying the Allies Rome would increase morale at home, stop the retreat of the German Army, and prove to the World that Germany was far from beaten. Hitler ordered a stand to be made south of Rome.

The German Defences at the Winter Line and the Scorched Earth Policy

The Germans, using forced Italian labour, immediately began building a system of defences to complement the already fantastic natural obstacles of gullies, mountains, winding roads and fast-flowing rivers. The natural terrain was made even more forbidding by the winter rains and snow that swelled or flooded the rivers and the mud.

The ground chosen by the German generals was amongst the most rugged and difficult and where the Italian peninsula was only 140 km across.It was a region with few roads. Into this area the German engineers,

(PAC PA115190)

Dead German Machine gunner, killed during German counter-attack at San Leonardo, Dec 10, 1943.

(PAC PA114482)

Canadian soldiers under sniper fire, Italy, October, 1943.

using more than 6,000 Italian civilians as forced labourers, built anti-tank ditches, strung barbed wire, planted 75,000 mines, set booby-traps, and constructed concrete strong-points and machine-gun nests. The whole system was designed in depth, often 10 or more km deep.

To add to their constructed positions the Germans employed their genius for demolition. They blew-up or collapsed 6,665 metres of tunnel, 12,210 metres of bridge, and uprooted or disabled almost 700,000 metres of railway. As part of their scorched earth policy, they created landslides, cratered roads, destroyed villages, and drove the unwanted refugees into the Allied lines. Anything that could be of use to the Allies was eliminated. The position was known as the Winter Line or the Bernhard Line. Every position had a clear field of fire. The soldiers manning the line were experienced troops, many of whom were veterans of the bloody fighting in Russia or in North Africa. The Allies "must" be stopped and these new positions would stop all but the bravest. Now the real fighting for Italy would begin.

The Plan to take Rome

The Allies planned to take Rome by having the Fifth Army attack directly towards Rome drawing away as many German troops as possible. The Eighth Army would then fake an attack on German positions in the Apennine mountains and then deliver the real blow on the Adriatic coastal plain. In the plan the Eighth Army would crack the German positions along the coast, sweep north and attack Rome from the north-east. This would force the Germans to abandon Rome and retreat or be encircled.

The Canadians were to support the Eighth Army's attack by trying to divert the Germans by threatening the outpost positions of the Bernhard Line. This itself was not going to be easy. The terrain that greeted the Canadians was one of blasted roads or roads blocked by landslides, burned villages, demolished buildings, gullies and woods. (The work of the Royal Canadian Engineers in constructing bridges, repairing roads and clearing mines was exceptional throughout the campaign.) Throughout November they pushed into the mountains. The Germans had set fire to many of the villages in the area and forced the homeless to flee towards the Allies, causing congestion on the narrow roads and supply problems. The winter conditions also affected the men. They were often unprepared for the extreme cold and heavy rain, and the scorched earth policy had deprived them of any winter accommodation. The going was slow.

The Battle of the Sangro River

General Bernard Montgomery, commander the Eighth Army launched his attack against the Bernhard Line on the night of November 28th/29th, 1943. Montgomery used British, Indian and New Zealander troops. His men successfully stormed the Sangro, and in two days of heavy fighting against well entrenched and experienced forces captured the ridge on the north side of the Sangro. He had cracked the Winter Line, as he had predicted, but the breakthrough "Monty" had hoped for did not materialize.

"We shall now hit the Germans a colossal crack."
General Bernard Montgomery, Commanding the Eight Army. Instructions to his generals for the upcoming assault on the Bernhard Line.

On December 1st/2nd the 1st Canadian Division was asked to take its place in the line. By the 4th they were overlooking the Moro River valley. A few small patrols had even crossed it. On the 6th they were joined by the 1st Canadian Armoured Brigade. Their mission was to cross the Moro, break the German lines and capture the port of Ortona. Canada's time had come.

The Battle of the Moro River

As the Canadians moved into their positions overlooking the Moro River they could observe the landscape beyond. They could see small farms, olive groves and vineyards that dotted the plain and the indents of the gullies and ravines that crossed it. The bridges that had crossed over them were all destroyed and the few roads that existed were in very poor condition. Those placid fields were mined and observed by enemy machine-guns. Dug into the gullies and ravines were the Germans, waiting for the Canadians to advance.

"...the ground was widely sown with S-mines, our abbreviation for Schuminen, deadly little wooden boxes filled with explosive which, when stepped on, sent a shower of metal pellets up between the legs..."
Major Strome Galloway, Royal Canadian Regiment.

Battleground Before Ortona By Lawren Harris.

Their goal was to attack across a six km stretch of the river valley and advance 3 km to Ortona. To undertake the assault they had close to 20,000 men. Even with artillery support and tanks this would be no easy mission. They were up against a fresh, experienced German force, who were no longer fighting a delaying action, but were to hold to the last man.

The first objective of the Canadian assault was to cross the Moro River in force and to establish a bridgehead large enough to accommodate the men and material to push through to Ortona. On December 6th, 1943, under the cover of darkness, and without any preliminary bombardment to help achieve surprise, three Canadian regiments (The Hastings and Prince Edward, The Seaforth Highlanders of Canada and The Princess Patricia's Canadian Light Infantry) crossed the Moro at three separate points, roughly two km apart. The men were unsure of the reception they would get, but before long they realized they had surprised no one. By morning all three groups had become pinned down by German mortar and sniper fire, but still managed to hold on to some of their gains. The Nazis responded quickly to the intrusion, and counter-attacked with infantry and tanks through the olive groves. The attacks were repulsed leaving many German dead and smoking tanks amongst the shattered trees.

In the end only the bridgehead near the Adriatic coast, created by the Hastings and Prince Edward Regiment (Hasty Ps), would be expanded and become an important "jump-off" position later in the battle.

Over the next few days men of the 1st Division continued to gain ground. They had established that their unseen enemy was not going to break, and that their positions would be defended ruthlessly. If they lost those positions, they would counter-attack again and again to retake them. The Canadian strategy responded to this German attitude. The Canadian attacks would have to be flexible, taking advantage of any apparent weakness along the German line. The strategy also focussed on particular strong points, often small places or cross-roads, whose significance to the German defensive system was far beyond their appearance on a map. The fighting before Ortona became just that: a battle of small places that were crucial to a certain part of the defence.

The first of these "small places" was the village of San Leonardo. It was the most important position guarding the line of the Moro River. To secure the required bridgehead it had to be taken.

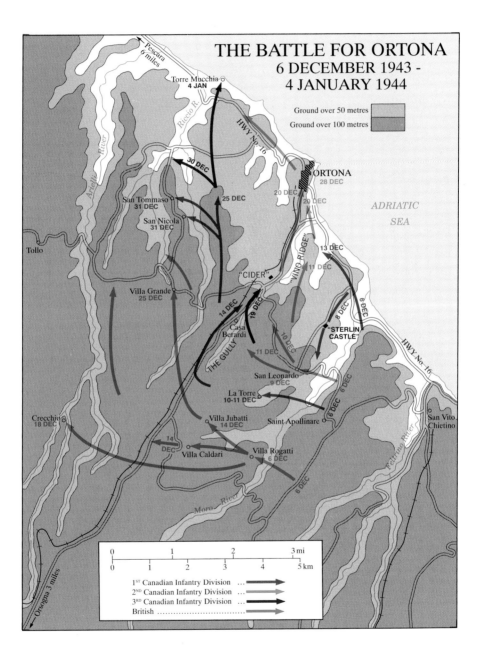

THE BATTLE FOR ORTONA
6 DECEMBER 1943 -
4 JANUARY 1944

Ground over 50 metres
Ground over 100 metres

Pescara
6 miles

Torre Mucchia
4 JAN

ORTONA
28 DEC

ADRIATIC
SEA

San Tommaso
31 DEC

25 DEC

San Nicola
31 DEC

Tollo

"VINO RIDGE"

13 DEC

11 DEC

"CIDER"

Villa Grande
25 DEC

14 DEC

19 DEC

Casa
Berardi

"STERLIN
CASTLE"

10 DEC

"THE GULLY"

11 DEC

San Leonardo
9 DEC

La Torre
10-11 DEC

Crecchio
18 DEC

Villa Jubatti
14 DEC

Saint Apollinare

San Vito
Chietino

14
DEC

Villa Caldari

Villa Rogatti
6 DEC

Moro River

Osogna 3 miles

| 0 | | 1 | | 2 | | 3 mi |
| 0 | 1 | 2 | 3 | 4 | | 5 km |

1ST Canadian Infantry Division ...
2ND Canadian Infantry Division ...
3RD Canadian Infantry Division ...
British ....

The Battle for San Leonardo, December 8th/9th, 1943

The plan for taking the village called for two Regiments, the Royal Canadian Regiment and the 48th Highlanders of Canada, to strike out three km apart, with the 48th attacking just west of the village and the RCR moving out of the Hasty Ps bridgehead and attacking in a southerly direction down the road leading to San Leonardo, three km distant. If both attacks succeeded the village would be outflanked, and in all probability the Germans would abandon it. Other Canadian troops and their armour would be waiting to exploit any opportunity offered by the advance.

"Welcome to sunny Italy."
A sarcastic greeting for reinforcements arriving in the mud and rain.

The weather throughout December was terrible. It rained and rained. This not only made life difficult for the soldiers, but a low cloud cover also meant no preliminary air strikes as the aircraft would be grounded. Fortunately for the Canadians, in advance of their assault on San Leonardo, 180 sorties by fighter-bombers softened the German positions. So on the morning of December 8th as the men started their advance towards San Leonardo, they must have been greatly relieved knowing the enemy's positions had been thoroughly blasted.

The 48th moved out, rapidly advanced one km and by the evening was firmly entrenched on their objective. Artillery fire had greatly supported the assault, and the Highlanders had performed well.

The assault of the RCR had to be delayed when the Germans launched a counter-attack against the bridgehead. The Canadians fought it off but it delayed the RCR attack, until 3 pm. Over the next few hours the men slowly pushed the Germans back, gradually advancing one km before a heavy bombardment and mortar fire forced them back. They ended up holding a small farmhouse on the road, only half way to San Leonardo.

After the attack was launched, the Royal Canadian Engineers went to work preparing the Moro River bed so the armour could get across and up the steep embankment. One engineer operated his bulldozer under heavy fire cutting a path for the tanks through the river bank. Gradually the tanks moved into action. They were a welcome relief to the soldiers. The tanks from The Calgary Regiment broke into San Leonardo accompanied by men of the Seaforth Highlanders. The small Canadian force dislodged the enemy and took the village. The Germans launched a counter-attack using 12 tanks and infantry. In a bloody fight the Canadians destroyed several of the tanks and shot down many Germans as they charged across the fields.

The few remaining men of the RCR who still held their positions were counter-attacked by the Nazis on December 9th. The German soldiers attacked with fanaticism, and in the end tried to kill every Canadian in the farmhouse on the San Leonardo road. Eleven men, under Lieutenant Sterlin, fought back. German dead were crumpled against the outside walls of the building; men were shot trying to throw grenades through the windows but in the end Sterlin and his men prevailed. They had more determination and courage than the Nazi attackers. From that point on the little farmhouse was known as Sterlin Castle.

The Germans launched one more vicious counter-attack against the Hasty Ps' bridgehead but were driven back by artillery and machine-gun fire. The Nazis stubbornly continued the attack but were no match for the Canadian firepower. Finally they retreated, leaving their dead scattered on the battlefield. With San Leonardo firmly in Canadian hands the Germans conceded the Moro River line to the victorious 1st Division. It had been their first real battle and was their first real victory.

"When the firing died down on our sector, stretcher and burial parties scouring the slimy slopes and tangles of shell-torn debris found 170 German corpses. Our own dead and wounded amounted to a third of the 400 or so Hasty Pees who had gone into the valley of the shadow."
Lieutenant Farley Mowat, Hastings and Prince Edward Regiment.

The Gully

No sooner had the enemy retired from the Moro River Line than they were busy fortifying a gully that was only two km away. The Gully ran parallel to the Moro and was only one km south of Ortona. It seemed that the whole operation would have to start all over again. Once again the Canadians would have to come up with a flexible plan that would ultimately reveal the next small place, the key to unlock The Gully's defences.

Once the Germans had retreated from the Moro the Canadians wasted no time in bringing across the fighting elements of the 1st Canadian

Division and the 1st Armoured Brigade. The weather had continued to deteriorate and steady rain had turned the entire region into a sea of yellow goo. All motorized vehicles, armoured cars and tanks were getting bogged down. The weather was also affecting the health of the battle-weary men and many were unable to fight. The Sick Lists were growing.

Allowing for as little time as possible for the Germans to prepare, the Canadians called for heavy air strikes on The Gully, and through to December 10th the Allied air superiority punished the enemy positions. At the same time men of the Loyal Edmonton Regiment, accompanied by tanks, pushed on from San Leonardo attacking a cross-roads on the north or German side of The Gully. The Loyal Eddies made good progress but, as they approached, German anti-tank, artillery and mortar fire drove them back. Reinforced by the 48th Highlanders and machine-guns of the Saskatoon Light Infantry they held on to some of their gains. The Gully was certainly going to be a prickly objective.

It was a natural defensive position, being six km long and about half a km wide where it met the sea. It was too wide to attack frontally, as any armour crossing it would be observed and destroyed in short order. It also had very deep sides which meant German positions dug into the other side of the banks would be immune from artillery fire. So only high-trajectory mortars would be an effective method of knocking out the German emplacements. The area was also rife with anti-tank mines and booby-traps. And the mud was stopping the tanks.

For these reasons the Canadians decided against a frontal assault on The Gully. Instead they decided first to secure the southern approaches to it and then outflank it on the west. On December 11th, 1943 the Princess Patricia's Canadian Light Infantry with tanks attacked and seized a ridge south of The Gully, known as Vino Ridge. It was a successful operation with few casualties. However on the same day other Canadians tried to get across it and capture a cross-roads, known as "Cider", south-east of Ortona. The attack failed. Over the next few days, fresh Canadian troops arrived and tried their hand at taking "Cider". On December 11th the West Nova Scotia Regiment attacked the west end of The Gully and were driven back. Artillery pounded the position on the 13th and the Carleton and York Regiment tried and failed in the face of mortars and machine-guns. To make matters worse low clouds prevented air strikes. Gradually the ranks were being depleted. The Canadians needed a break.

Casa Berardi by Charles F. Comfort.   (CWM 12255)

The break came when a small group of 40 Seaforth Highlanders with four tanks managed to find a way to slip through the German defences. This small band of men surprised a Nazi garrison and captured 78 prisoners. Unfortunately they could not be reinforced and had to withdraw. But they had found the key to The Gully's defence. It appeared the German line was vulnerable two km west of a small place called Casa Berardi.

Casa Berardi was on the main road to Ortona, and only one km from the vital "Cider" cross-roads. The plan was for the Royal 22e Regiment to attack towards the Ortona road, and once the road was reached turn northeast and follow the road to Casa Berardi, thereby turning the flank of the German positions in The Gully. It was to be a tough task, and only the most courageous effort by the most dedicated men could pull it off.

Casa Berardi

At 7:30 am on December 14th, 1943 the men of the Royal 22e Regiment, the "Van Doos", moved out accompanied by seven tanks of The Ontario Regiment. Canadian artillery had pounded the enemy's positions to assist the advance. What attackers did not know was that the enemy had also identified this area as vulnerable and had reinforced it. The troops who held the line were now fresh and were members of an elite formation, the Parachute Regiment.

The advance of the Van Doos was immediately held up by a concealed German tank. But individual courage took hold and, one soldier courageously dashed across an open field and using a PIAT anti-tank weapon shot the tank at point-blank range. The tank exploded and the turret was flung into the air. It was now 10:30 am and the small force was joined by the tanks and once again moved to the attack and quickly reached the Ortona road.

The Nazis were well dug in but the tenacity of the Canadian attack was too much for them. The Sherman tanks of The Ontario Regiment knocked out three Panzer Mark IV tanks, and the infantry eliminated strong points with grenades and rifle fire. German artillery was exploding all around the men and the attackers were reduced to only fifty. None-the-less they continued to advance, passing by Casa Berardi and getting closer to the "Cider" cross-roads. Caught in the open fields, the small force was being destroyed by German artillery and mortar fire. At their commander's urging they raced for the most protected place on the battlefield, the buildings of Casa Berardi. Once inside Captain Paul Triquet organized his force, now less than 15 men and four tanks, to defend their gains. With little ammunition and only a handful of light machine-guns Triquet's men had to hold on until reinforced or the day's sacrifices would be wasted.

"We're surrounded. The enemy is in front of us, behind us and on our flanks. The safest place is on the objective."
Captain Paul Triquet, VC, Royal 22e Regiment, urging his men forward in the face of heavy fire, near Casa Berardi.

At nightfall the small band was reinforced and in the darkness the Germans could no longer attack. The courageous work of Captain Paul Triquet, his band of Van Doos and tanks of The Ontario Regiment, had cracked the German line. For his exceptional courage and leadership at Casa Berardi Paul Triquet was later awarded the Victoria Cross, the British Commonwealth's highest award for bravery.

The success at Casa Berardi was quickly followed by the Canadians' preparation of defences to stop the anticipated Nazi counter-attacks. Some groups tried to improve the gains but were met by a torrent of fire from concealed German positions. When the final counter-attack did come it was crushed by Canadian artillery. Over the next few days patrols found that the Germans were retiring from The Gully, but that they still held the "Cider" crossroads leading to Ortona.

On the morning of December 18th, 1943 the largest artillery bombard-ment thus far in the campaign blasted the Germans around the "Cider" cross-roads. Canadian infantry, the 48th Highlanders in the vanguard, advanced into the smoke and dust through the olive groves and vineyards. Soon the enemy responded, but it was too late as the tanks of the Three Rivers Regiment dealt with the opposition.

The Royal Canadian Regiment was next to advance, under the cover of an enormous barrage, directly across The Gully towards the cross-roads. But their protective shelling was called off prematurely and the RCR were caught in the open and suffered heavy casualties after only advancing 100 metres. Amongst the RCR casualties in the fighting was Lieutenant Mitchell Sterlin whose courage was so important in the success of the ear-lier attacks. Sterlin died on December 19th.

(CWM 12231)

Battle Scene (Fantasy), Berardi Road by Charles F. Comfort.

"Enemy fire struck heavily as the troops crossed the start line... The barrage was called off. This allowed the enemy machine-gunners to pop up and bring their deadly weapons into play... "D" Company advancing along the Ortona road was reduced to a dozen men cowering in a roadside ditch."
Major Strome Galloway, Royal Canadian Regiment.

On the afternoon of December 19th the attack was renewed. This time all went according to plan and by the evening the "Cider" cross-roads were finally in Canadian hands. It had taken ten days for the Canadians with a force of almost 20,000 men, to advance a mere 2,300 metres. This statistic alone shows how vicious the fighting was and how tenacious the defence. The successes to this point in the fighting were a credit to the 1st Canadian Division. They had won a bitter victory. But the battle was not over yet.

The Battle for Ortona

On December 20th the Loyal Edmonton Regiment moved down from the "Cider" cross-roads towards Ortona. The road was mined and despite the efforts of engineers to clear the passage for the armour, four tanks were put out of action by well-concealed mines. Many in the advancing party and those back at Headquarters thought the Germans would abandon the old port without a fight. At dawn the Loyal Eddies reached the outskirts of the town. The Germans had not gone.

"Everything before Ortona was a nursery tale."
Major-General Chris Vokes, Commanding the 1st Canadian Division.

Ortona is an ancient sea port dating back over 3,000 years. It is a beautiful town located on a hook-shaped promontory over-looking the Adriatic. A 15th century castle dominates the skyline, and its streets are cobble-stoned and narrow (only the few main thoroughfares are wide enough for a tank to pass). Two and three story buildings line the sides of each street and all streets seem to lead to the main town squares at the San Tommasso cathedral or the Town Hall. It is the stuff of travel posters, not house-to-house fighting.

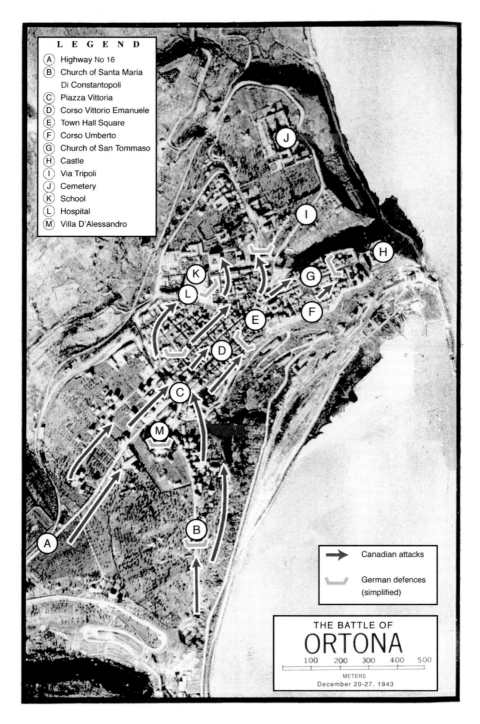

LEGEND
- (A) Highway No 16
- (B) Church of Santa Maria Di Constantopoli
- (C) Piazza Vittoria
- (D) Corso Vittorio Emanuele
- (E) Town Hall Square
- (F) Corso Umberto
- (G) Church of San Tommaso
- (H) Castle
- (I) Via Tripoli
- (J) Cemetery
- (K) School
- (L) Hospital
- (M) Villa D'Alessandro

→ Canadian attacks

German defences (simplified)

THE BATTLE OF
ORTONA
100 200 300 400 500
METERS
December 20-27, 1943

The population of the town in 1943 was 10,000 inhabitants. Until the Allied invasion and the surrender of Italy life had been good in Ortona. It was not until the end of September, when the Germans appeared and started to destroy the harbour facilities, that everything changed. The Germans were now the enemy and they could be ruthless. As the Allies advanced closer to Ortona the Germans rounded up all available Italians and forced them to work on the positions defending the Bernhard Line. A scarcity of food added to the civilians' woes. As the attacks came closer the Nazis became more oppressive and the inhabitants worked non-stop digging anti-tank ditches and trenches. At the end of November the civilians were driven from the town, but many stayed behind, hiding in basements and caves. For many this decision would cost them their lives.

As the Canadians cleared the German paratroopers from the "Cider" cross-roads, other paratroopers were systematically blowing up old buildings in Ortona so that they collapsed across the narrow streets, blocking them. The ancient cathedral of San Tommasso was reduced to rubble by the German demolition charges. Booby-traps were prepared, mines laid, and formidable defensive positions were created, designed to annihilate any attacker in vicious cross-fires. The Nazis chose the best positions for their artillery, mortars and machine-guns. It was these defences, and a determined foe that the Canadians would have to beat to take Ortona. In addition to the man-made positions, natural obstacles surrounded the port on three sides. The only way in was from the south-west. From this direction the Loyal Edmonton Regiment was from advancing at early light on December 21st, 1943, when the first shots in the battle for Ortona were fired.

The main group of Canadians (Edmontons, tanks of the Three Rivers Regiment, and supporting light anti-tank artillery and machine-guns) were moving along the Ortona road when the Germans opened fire from a strong-point at the Villa D'Alessandro. The ferocity of the explosions from incoming mortars and mines and the constant rattle of machine-guns checked the Edmontons. A second group of soldiers, the Seaforth Highlanders, made some progress on the coastal road, capturing a small port; but Paratroopers hiding in the Cathedral of Santa Maria di Constantinopoli and in the buildings on the edge of town kept a constant barrage of fire on them. Snipers made every move a potentially deadly one. The attack stalled but reinforcements accompanied by tanks and light artillery moved to help.

At the cathedral the Germans finally withdrew, but showed no signs of giving elsewhere. In the grounds of the Villa D'Alessandro the Eddies closed in and the fighting became building to building, face-to-face. By nightfall the Villa was in Canadian hands. The tenacious enemy had retired into the old city.

December 22nd, 1943

At dawn Sherman tanks of the Three Rivers Regiment rumbled into the Piazza Vittoria firing into the old buildings as they went. Most roads were blocked by the extensive demolitions, but the Shermans provided the infantry with important support. The Edmontons moved with the armour fighting alongside. Mines provided a constant hazard as did the German snipers, but slowly the way was cleared for the tanks. Small groups of men, armed with grenades and rifles took one house at a time. Close encounters with the Paratroopers, often unseen until the last second, marked each step forward. The small bands hunted each other through the rubble. Each house had to be approached cautiously, a grenade thrown through a window, the door kicked in, and the men would burst through firing. Grenades were rolled down stairs into basements. The smoke of the explosions and the smell of cordite in the air accentuated the fear and anxiety. The men would walk over the prostrate bodies of the bloodied paratroopers and move on to the next house.

Under fire Canadian Engineers would sweep the roads for mines, and clear them. But sniper fire from Nazis securely hidden in the upper stories of the houses was deadly accurate in close quarters. The tanks would assist the sappers by blasting the upper stories of the houses or wherever the enemy seemed to be hiding.

The going was slow down the main avenues. The Loyal Eddies and the Seaforths found moving in the streets deadly and on the side streets without tank support movement was virtually suicide. Light anti-tank guns (six pounders, named after the weight of the shell they fired) were rolled in to help the advance. At point-blank range they fired round after round trying to dislodge the entrenched Paratroopers. Soldiers would rush-up to follow the confusion created by the shelling and charge through the smoke and over the rubble into the buildings.

Not only Canadians and Germans were being killed in the fighting. There were still thousands of civilians in the city-those who had crept back into the town after the Nazis ordered them to leave. No one on either side knew where they may be hiding or when they may appear. In many ways they became innocent targets of both sides. After a few days of fighting hundreds had been killed in the shelling or crushed by collapsing buildings. They also provided an unhealthy distraction for the Canadians, as no one would want to hurt these people and in fact trying to help them could cost a soldier his life.

Gradually the Eddies moved down the main street towards a huge mound of rubble blocking the Corso Emanuele. The enemy had purposely blocked all roads leaving only this access open. They directed a devastating fire on the Canadian tanks. It was a crucial position for them to hold and they appeared to have succeeded in stopping the advance. It was near the roadblock that the fighting seemed to have ended on December 22nd. The Canadians had advanced roughly 600 metres into the town and were still 200 metres away from the Town Hall.

The Paratroopers now had a surprise for the Canadians as small groups worked their way through basements and holed walls through connecting buildings to come out behind the attackers. In the dark the Germans were defeated but this sudden change of events must have shaken the Canadians. Through the night the fighting continued and a small group of Edmontons, climbing over roofs, came out behind the enemy and captured the Town Hall. This brave action forced the Paratroopers to retreat from the roadblock and the Town Square, a place they had so securely held only a few hours before.

December 23rd, 1943

In the morning reinforcements arrived for the Canadians as more Seaforths joined the fighting. Shermans of the Three Rivers Regiment made their way over the roadblock only to find the Germans had blocked the exits out of the Town Hall Square. The Loyal Eddies moved out into the north-west part of Ortona. It was the oldest part of the city and would be very difficult to take. The Highlanders were given the task of attacking north-east, over a series of important roads, to capture the town cemetery. Neither unit could have looked forward to their assignments, but Ortona was important to the men. Taking it from the elite German Paratroopers became a point of honour.

The German defences they now faced were even more difficult because the narrow roads and the collapsed buildings reduced the ability

Ortona from the South. (PAC PA204298)

Infantry of The Edmonton Regiment, supported by Sherman tanks of The Three Rivers Regiment. Ortona, December 23, 1943. (PAC PA114030)

of tanks to assist. From here on in it was going to be Seaforth or Edmonton versus the Nazis. No one could advance down the street because of sniper and machine-gun fire and no house was safe. From here on in it was explosives, grenades and courage and a technique that was known as "mouse-holing".

"Mouse-holing" was a technique by which the soldiers avoided exposing themselves to the streets. They would move from house-to-house by blasting a hole through a wall leading into the next house. Once the hole was made the troops would rush through the smoke and debris and attack the enemy positions in the next house. House-by-house the Canadians were taking Ortona, and beating the Germans at their own game.

The Seaforths were struggling ahead through the Town Hall Square towards the cemetery. The Germans were defending the roads leading from the Town Square fearlessly and had stalled the attack. Even the arrival of the Shermans could not improve the situation. The fighting on the 23rd had changed little in Ortona, but it had increased the lists of dead and wounded.

December 24th, 1943

The pressure of the Canadian attacks in the city has depleted the Paratroopers ranks. More men arrived but the determined men of this elite force being reduced to a remnant. Bodies of the dead Germans lay sprawled on the rubble, and arms and legs protruded from piles of bricks. The cost had been high and they knew that as the Canadians captured more of the old city they were in danger of being cut off.

Outside of Ortona other Regiments of the 1st Canadian Division were trying to cut the town off by capturing positions north-west of it. These attacks were not wholly successful but concerned the Germans as they reduced their avenues of escape from town.

Ortona also became a focus for the international journalists. The struggle between the Canadians and the Nazis in the broken streets of the ancient town was front page news around the world. This spotlight did much for the profile of the Canadian soldiers and was a boost for morale. The attention focussed on the battle intensified the will of both sides to win.

Via Dolorosa-Ortona by Charles F. Comfort.   (CWM 12402)

Canadian artillery pounded the town on the 24th and the men from the Loyal Edmonton Regiment and the Seaforth Highlanders renewed their assaults. The resistance in the streets stiffened as more Paratroopers joined in the battle. The soldiers were back to "mouse-holing", from one house to another, coming face-to-face with the enemy. Adding to the terror the Germans were now using flame-throwers to roust out the Canadians. The explosions from rockets and mortars were wounding and killing many men and the Canadian artillery and mortars responded in kind. The noise of battle was deafening.

As the bloody fighting along the main road, the Corso Umberto, failed to dislodge the Nazis, the Eddies moved into the side streets to try and find a way around the enemy defences. In some places the fighting was hand-to-hand as a surprised group of Canadians fell upon an even more surprised group of Paratroopers. Prisoners were taken but it sometimes appeared optional. Most prisoners were those so badly wounded they could no longer resist. As the Canadians came across civilians in the battle they were surprised to be treated as liberators Amidst the terror and death the trapped refugees wanted to celebrate. Some of the Italians led the soldiers through the maze of debris to hidden German positions. But with Christmas Eve approaching many felt their plight was hopeless.

The fighting continued as tanks opened a way for the Canadian infantry to take a school and advance 100 metres, but the German resistance was not weakening, and the rubble seemed to go on forever.

Christmas Day, December 25th, 1943

On Christmas Day the fighting in and around Ortona abated, but did not stop. Within the sound of rifle and mortar fire the Seaforths had a table-set dinner at the Cathedral of San di Constantanopoli, a place they had captured only a few days before. The Edmontons were still in the city and had little respite. They did have Christmas dinners delivered to them in the lines. Certainly the faith of the men was to be tested this Christmas. By Ortona standards, Christmas, 1943, was a very quiet day.

(PAC PA114032)

Ortona, December 1943.

(PAC PA130308)

Ruins of the Cathedral of San Tommaso, December 1943.

"Outside our building men were dying. In the muddy vineyards they found their place on earth - the Christmas message through the ages. But they didn't hear any angels sing, only the stutter of machine-guns, the crack of rifles, and the screaming, whining and thudding of shells and mortar bombs. They were as far from Bethlehem as Man could get."
Major Strome Galloway, Royal Canadian Regiment.

December 26th, 1943

On the 26th the Loyal Edmontons renewed their assault towards the old castle and pushed towards the Square of the San Tommasso Cathedral. The Germans were hanging on everywhere. Their machine-gun nests clung to every pile of rubble and their anti-tank guns covered the approaches to the Square firing deadly volleys at the Shermans, who could do little to move out of the way in the narrow, debris-filled streets. But the enemy was still fighting back with deadly tricks. A group of 24 Eddies was in a recently captured building. The Paratroopers had mined it prior to retreating, and once they knew the Canadians were inside blew the charges and collapsed the building. The 24 men were trapped and either were crushed or suffocated. This added fuel to the Canadian attacks and the Eddies would get revenge by collapsing a three-story building on an unsuspecting party of 50 Nazis. All were killed.

December 26th was a good day for the Edmontons and the Seaforths who together captured the San Tommasso Square and a school that had held out for days. The enemy quickly withdrew, collapsing buildings behind them. It was a war of cunning and courage and it was a battle the Canadians were winning. Each metre forward came closer to cutting the Germans off in the town, and the Germans knew it. The Paratroopers holding the old castle knew if the Seaforths advanced much further they would be trapped.

December 27th, 1943

Overnight on December 27th the Germans planted mines in many of the recently vacated buildings, and blew them when they could see Canadians moving into them. But the battle continued, the men threw grenades into a house, and then sprung through the door blasting anything in the way. The fighting was hard near the San Tommasso Square, but in many ways it was too late for the Germans. The tide of the battle had shifted to the Canadians, and now they were hunting the Paratroopers.

Off the Adriatic coast of Ortona Allied naval ships were coming along side and shelling the Germans in the old castle and in the Town Cemetery. This attack killed many and diverted attention from the Canadian attacks. Outside the castle the Edmontons were moving in, and in the Via Roma, the road to the cemetery, the Seaforths were also winning forward. If the Seaforths could reach the cemetery they would cut-off the Germans in Ortona.

By nightfall the Paratroops realized they were beaten, and decided to leave Ortona. Remnants of two Paratroop battalions, only a handful of men, left the town under the cover of darkness. They had taken a severe beating. The next morning, December 28th, the Canadians found the Germans gone. The Battle for Ortona was over. The Canadians had won.

During the Battle for Ortona the Loyal Edmonton Regiment used: 918 anti-tank shells, 6,050 mortar shells. 57,000 rifle bullets, 700 smoke grenades and 600 hand grenades.

In the following days the Canadians started the grim work of recovering the dead, and clearing the mines and rubble. On one of the side streets the men were digging out the bodies of the 24 Loyal Eddies who were crushed when the Nazis collapsed a building on them. One by one the corpses were exhumed, but one of the men heard a moan. There were survivors. Frantically they dug. It had been more than three days since the men had been trapped so every second counted. Finally they found one of their comrades alive. Lance Corporal Roy Boyd had managed to survive after all this time. It was a miracle.

"It is like coming back from the dead."
Lance Corporal Roy Boyd, Loyal Edmonton Regiment. The sole survivor of 24 Eddies trapped in a collapsed building.

(CWM 12245)

Tank Amid Ruins by Charles F. Comfort

"We collected all our own dead all right but when it came to the Jerries we made a half hearted attempt to dig graves. But the weather was cold and the ground was frozen, so to Hell with it. We gathered them all up and heaved them down a well and heaved a hand grenade down with them. A real Vikings' funeral."
An Anonymous soldier, Seaforth Highlanders of Canada.

"... on a pile of rubble, precariously balanced, killed by an anti-tank gun and set on fire, was perched a Canadian tank. Near the tank was the gun that killed it, its crew of two blown to pieces. There were dozens of mines lying about and a careless step meant death... There was smoke here, there, and everywhere. And flames, and the dead."
Matthew Halton, Canadian War Correspondent.

The fighting since the Crossing of the Moro River at the beginning of December had cost the Canadians 2,339 killed, wounded and missing. In the fighting for Ortona alone the Canadians suffered 650 casualties, mostly to the Seaforths and the Edmontons. They lost 144 (41 killed) and 172 (63 killed) respectively. The ratio of wounded to killed is a cold, but significant indication of the severity of a battle. Normally it is roughly 10:1, but at Ortona it was closer to 2:1. That signifies a brutal battle. German losses are more difficult to determine, but they lost at least as many and probably more than the Canadians. The saddest casualties were those of the Italian civilians killed and wounded in the fighting. It has been estimated more than 1,300 were killed.

The Battle for Ortona ended the Italian Campaign for 1943. A few patrols pushed north of the city in the New Year, but the men were exhausted from the continuous fighting and the cold winter weather had made the ground impassable. The bloody road to Rome was still blocked and would not be opened for another six months.

The "Spaghetti League" turned to a bloody war of attrition, that spawned such battles as the infamous Monte Cassino, Anzio and a host of others. Italy was no soft underbelly to be pierced, it was a brutally difficult country in which to fight, defended by an experienced, fanatical enemy.

The Canadian forces in Italy would be increased in 1944, and the Canadians would see more hardship in places known as the Gothic Line, Rimini, Ravenna and the Po. Those places would become too well known to most Canadians because so many men died there.

In all 92,527 Canadians would serve in the Italian Campaign, 1943-1945. Of those 26,254 or 28% would become casualties. Five thousand and three hundred and ninety-nine would never come home. They rest in the well-kept Canadian War Cemeteries in Sicily and Italy. They rest near the cemeteries of the British, Americans, New Zealanders, Indians and Poles who died with them in "Sunny Italy". Their sacrifices to stop the world's greatest tyrant, Adolf Hitler, should never be forgotten.

The Sicilian and Italian Campaigns gave the Canadian soldiers an opportunity to prove themselves, which they did with great courage and determination. Before long they were veterans of war. Their successes built up morale, and enhanced their reputation. But the fighting from the Moro and in Ortona gave them something else, their first hard-won victory.

"...the 1st Canadian Division proved itself equal to the grim role it was cast in. Confronted with one of the toughest, bloodiest battles of the Italian campaign, this great Canadian formation earned a full share of glory, in their valiant struggle, not only for the liberation of Ortona, but for the political and spiritual freedom which is the supreme ideal of western civilization and western culture."

Charles Comfort, Canadian War Artist.

Bibliography - Suggested Reading

The Canadians in Italy, 1943-1945 by G.W.L. Nicholson. Queen's Printer,1957.

1943: The Road To Ortona by Saverio Di Tullio. Legas, 1998.

Artist At War by Charles Comfort. The Ryerson Press. Toronto, 1956.

Bravely into Battle by Strome Galloway. Stoddart, 1988.

The Regiment by Farley Mowat. McClelland & Stewart, 1955.

And No Bird Sang by Farley Mowat. McClelland & Stewart, 1979.

Ortona by Mark Zuehlke. Stoddart, 1999